W9-DAU-134

5-8

What Can Live in the Mountains?

by Sheila Anderson

first step nonfiction

Lerner Publications Company · Minneapolis

A mountain is a **habitat**.

It is where plants and
animals live.

Mountain animals have special **adaptations**.

These help them live on mountains.

Pikas use long teeth to bite off plants.

They save them to eat during winter.

Golden eagles have sharp **talons**.

They use them to catch
small animals.

Yaks grow thick fur **coats**.

They keep them warm in the winter.

The long tails of snow
leopards help them land
after they leap.

Their gray and black coats help them blend in with the mountains.

Bighorn sheep jump on the rocks.

Their split **hooves** help them grip the ground and rocks.

Mountain lions have strong legs for leaping.

What other adaptations
help animals live in the
mountains?   17

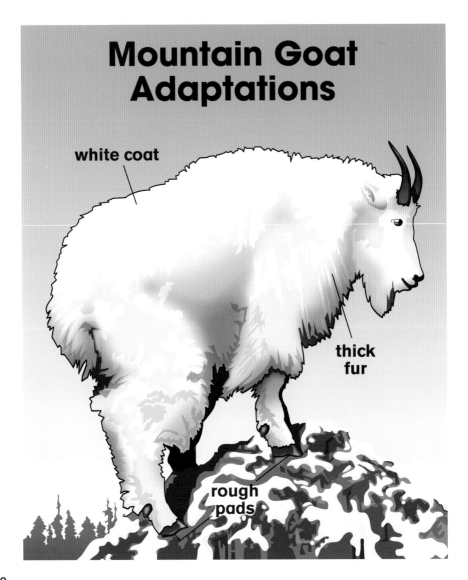

Mountain Goat Adaptations

white coat

thick fur

rough pads

Learn More about Adaptations

Mountain goats have thick coats of fur that keep them warm during cold winters. Their white color helps them blend in with their snowy surroundings. Rough pads on the bottom of their feet help them grip jagged rocks. Cool!

Fun Facts

 Llamas have large lungs that help them breathe the thin mountain air.

 Mountain birds and spiders eat insects that have been blown up the mountains by the wind.

 Eagles use their long wings to soar on mountain breezes. They save energy by riding the wind.

 Weasels have narrow bodies that can fit in tight spaces between rocks.

 Condors are mountain birds. They eat animals that have fallen to their deaths.

 Yaks have two layers of fur to keep them warm in the winter.

 Snow leopards have large, hairy feet that help them walk on top of the snow.

Glossary

 adaptations – things that help a plant or animal live in a specific habitat

 coat – a layer of fur

 habitat – a place to live

 hooves – hard coverings on the feet of some animals

 talon – a bird's claw

Index

The images in this book are used with the permission of: © Mike Norton/Shutterstock Images, pp. 2, 22 (center); © Marli Miller/Visuals Unlimited, Inc., p. 3; © Joseph Van Os/The Image Bank/Getty Images, pp. 4, 22 (top); © Richard Thom/Visuals Unlimited, Inc., p. 5; © John Cancalosi/NHPA/Photoshot, p. 6; © Thomas Kitchin & Victoria Hurst/NHPA/Photoshot, p. 7; © Mark Hamblin/Photoshot, pp. 8, 22 (bottom); © Laurie Campbell/NHPA/Photoshot, p. 9; © Bryan and Cherry Alexander/NHPA/Photoshot, pp. 10, 22 (second from top); © A.N.T. Photo Library/NHPA/Photoshot, p. 11; © WILDLIFE/Peter Arnold, Inc., p. 12; © Biosphoto/Klein J.-L. & Hubert M.-L./Peter Arnold, Inc., p. 13; © AllCanadaPhotos/Photoshot, pp. 14, 15, 22 (second from bottom); © Daisy Gilardini/The Image Bank/Getty Images, p. 16; © Steve Knell/naturepl.com, p. 17; © Laura Westlund/Independent Picture Service, p. 18.

Front cover: © Photodisc/Getty Images.

Lerner Publications Company
A division of Lerner Publishing Group, Inc.
241 First Avenue North
Minneapolis, MN 55401 U.S.A.

Website address: www.lernerbooks.com

Library of Congress Cataloging-in-Publication Data

Anderson, Sheila.
    What can live in the mountains? / by Sheila Anderson.
       p.   cm. — (First step nonfiction. Animal adaptations)
    Includes index.
    ISBN 978-0-7613-4572-5 (lib. bdg. : alk. paper)
    1. Mountain animals—Adaptation—Juvenile literature. I. Title.
QL113.A53 2011
591.75'3—dc22   2009025208

Manufactured in the United States of America
1 – DP – 7/15/10